In Celebration of Friendship

Other Books by Rusty Berkus

Life Is A Gift
Appearances
To Heal Again
Soulprints
Nell The Nebbish

Library of Congress Card Number: 90-60836

ISBN 0-9609888-8-2

Published by Red Rose Press
P.O. Box 2212
Santa Monica, CA 90401

First Edition

First Printing

In Celebration of Friendship

illustrated by Jan Salerno

by Rusty Berkus

Red Rose Press
Santa Monica, California
1990

with love to my daughter Cami
and my son and daughter-in-law, Steve and Tracy

Fresh from the womb, inherent in our first cry,
is the primal call for love.

Another's eyes behold our eyes,
another's heart bonds to our heart,
another's arms enfold our arms.

It is from this first enjoinment
that the seeds of all subsequent friendships
will be sown.

Rusty Berkus

Of the billions of people on the planet
it is no accident that you and I were brought together
to forever affect each other's lives

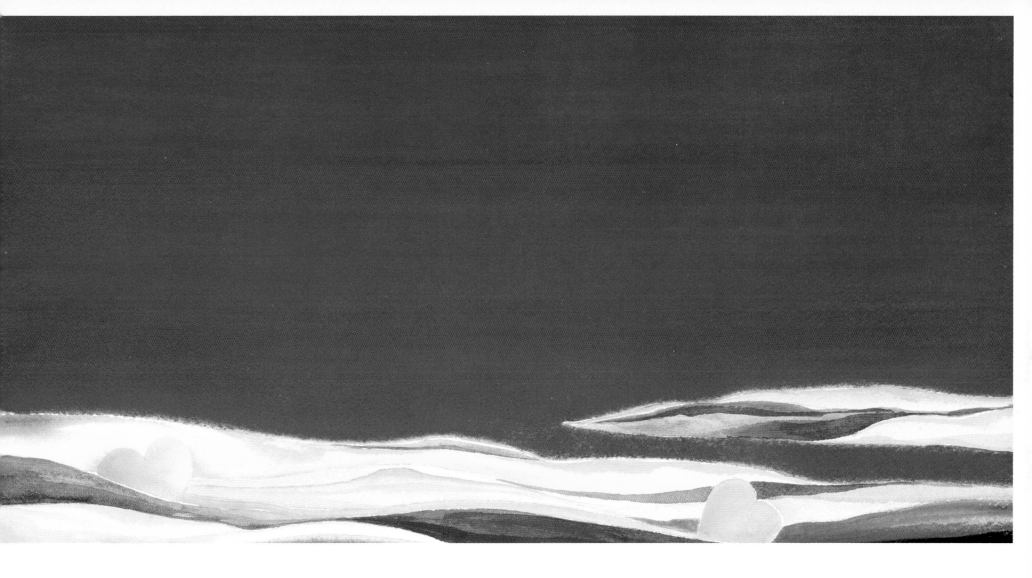

From the familiar strangeness of our meeting
came an invisible bonding.

From the one small seed of our first encounter
has come many harvests.

We have journeyed together through the tender terrain of each other's feelings
where there has been no map or compass to guide us.

We have wandered through the wilderness of uncertainty
where fear was sometimes the stranger between us.

Only to come upon a clearing
          where we were sunsplashed in the warmth
          of the honesty between us.

From time to time,
 we have moved in and out of each other's lives,
  as naturally as the leaves fall away from a tree
   during its cycle of seasons.

You have heard me
    when no one else took the time to listen.

You have seen me
    when no one took the time to find me.

You have made it safe for the child in me
to dance my dance and sing my song
to my own unique rhythm and rhyme.

We have lived the joy of each other's finest hours,
and sat together in silent vigil
during our darkest moments.

It is through our kinship
    that I have learned to give and receive,
        to forgive and accept forgiveness.

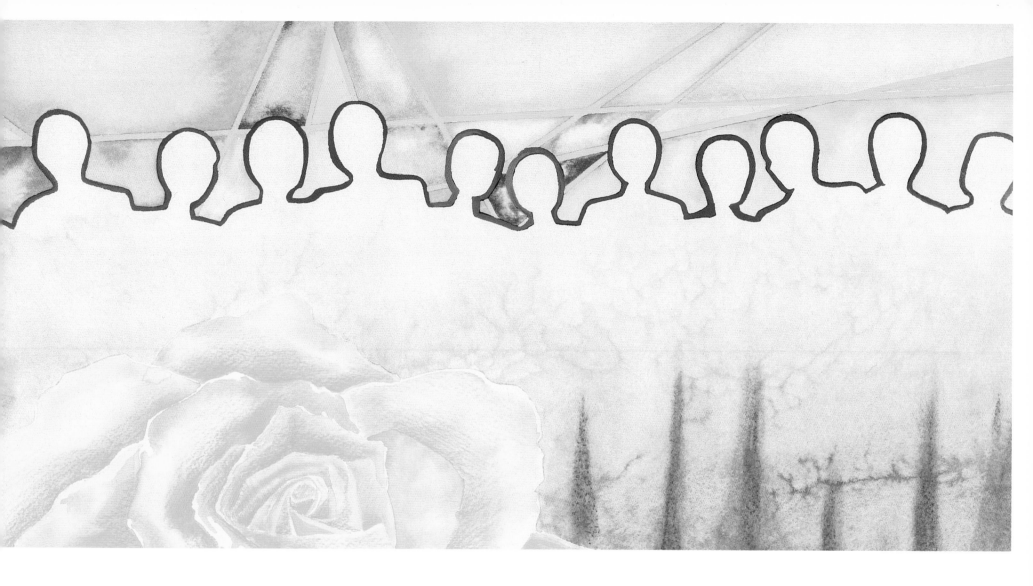

Enabling my kinship with others
to be one of giving and receiving,
forgiving and accepting forgiveness.

We have loved each other for our shadows
as well as our sunlight.

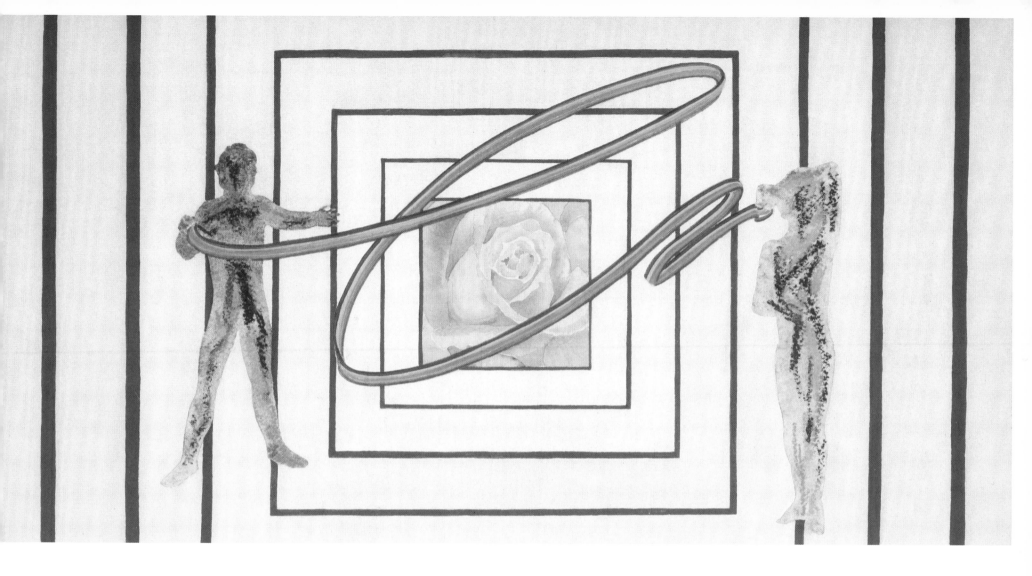

Sharing a world within the world,
    a holy sanctuary,
        where we could be as innocent children–
      defenseless and thereby safe,
       fearless and thereby free.

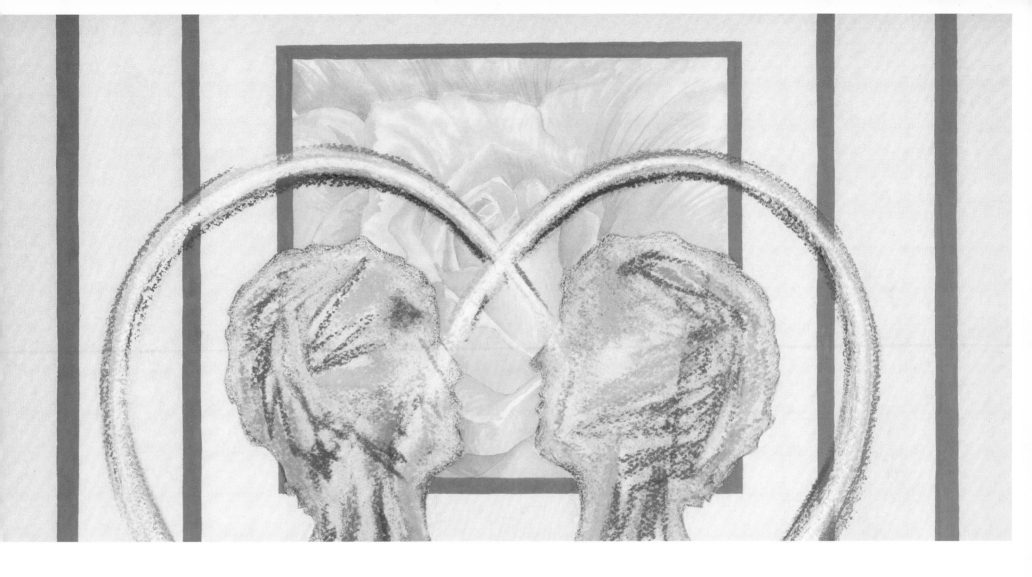

It is in this refuge that dignity is restored,
more of our preciousness is discovered,
and we are mended in the broken places.

It is here that we are able to dream the dreams
that make all things seem possible.

Here, darkness is dispelled for a time,
and ideas of greatness are born.

It is in this world that we can dare to imagine
the door to our greatness opening.

This world within the world is a sacred place
where all are welcome
who come in the name of love.

The history we have together
can never be erased by time
nor distance.

For I know that I am never alone–
    never will be alone,
        no matter where you are in the world.

I am able to remind others of their own inherent majesty,
because you have made it possible for me
to remember who I am.

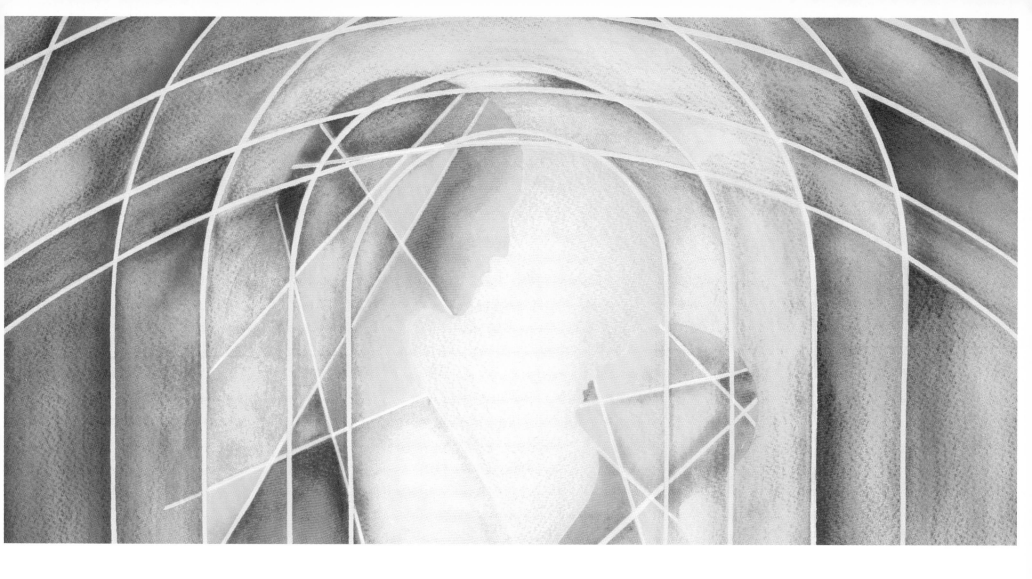

For it is the look on the face of the Other
that gives us our sense of Self.

Relationships are everything.

About the Author

Rusty Berkus is a poet, composer, lyricist and has her Masters Degree in Marriage and Family Counseling. However, she is most proud of being a mother, daughter and friend.

Rusty feels that inherent in the anatomy of all relationships are the qualities of heartiness and vulnerability, which are in juxtaposition to each other.

"A friendship must be given adequate amounts of light, air and water, just as one would tend a beautiful garden. Light is a form of energy representing the time and attention given to the relationship. Air symbolizes the ability to allow the relationship space to breathe. Water becomes the spiritual element in which a kind of baptism takes place where the relationship is in a continuous cycle of renewal and purification through awareness and communication."

Rusty believes that love is the most powerful healing force in the universe. For those who place a high priority on the quality of their relationships, happiness is inevitable.

About the Illustrator

Jan Salerno is a visionary artist, printmaker and graphic designer working in Los Angeles. "Through our relationships we are initiated into our star selves. Dancing with our mirrors, dreaming on our reflections, we awaken to the power of love and create transformation."

This book is dedicated to those friends
who have listened to my dreams
and who have enabled me to make them come true.